Transformed Women in the Bible

Explore Real Life Issues
Experience Real Life Change

Julie-Allyson Ieron

wesleyan
publishing
house

Indianapolis, Indiana

Copyright © 2006 by Wesleyan Publishing House
Published by Wesleyan Publishing House
Indianapolis, Indiana 46250
Printed in the United States of America

ISBN-13: 978-0-89827-339-7
ISBN-10: 0-89827-339-0

To the Reader

I write to you as a friend—as a fellow journeyer on the trek toward knowing God in new and intimate ways. Like you, I'm busy. I'm often overwhelmed and frequently weary. I don't need one more assignment to add to my long to-do list that would take well into the second Tuesday of next week to complete. And yet, I have a longing to know God—who He is, what He wants from me, what He has planned for me. As part of that longing, I've been getting to know the many women whose stories appear in His Word. In knowing them—how they came to faith, how they lived their lives, how they interacted with the God of the universe—I have come to understand many new truths about the real purpose God had when He created woman. And I have come to understand something about the real purpose God had when He created you and me.

So, I invite you on this journey of discovery. We'll meet women who had families, women who had a message from God, women who felt the hand of God's Son on their lives. We'll also meet women who faced tragic and trying circumstances, women who made some questionable decisions, and women who found God faithful and true to His word. In short, we'll meet sisters in faith who faced the same struggles we face.

This is a practical journey, one that has a great deal of relevance to the lives we live in this day. So, alongside the stories of Bible women, you'll read brief snippets from women of our millennium—women of faith from all walks of life who are demonstrating what it means to put Bible lessons into practice.

You may choose to take this journey alone or as part of a small group or Bible class. If you take it alone, I challenge you to find a trusted friend who can help you process the decisions you'll make along the way—someone who can help hold you accountable before God for the commitments you'll make to living in a closer and deeper relationship with His Son, Jesus Christ.

If you choose to take this journey as part of a regular group meeting, take some time before going to your meeting to read the brief introductory sections, "For Openers" and "Getting to Know Her," as well as the primary Scripture passage for that week's session.

By taking a few moments out of your week to prepare your heart, you'll find a richer and fuller experience all along the way.

So, come on. Let me introduce you to some amazing sisters, women who touched the heart of God.

To the Leader

I hope you're excited about beginning this journey together. The women of the Bible have so much to teach us as women of the twenty-first century. Their homes and conveniences might have looked different, but their challenges were much like ours. They experienced the stress of raising a family, the frustration of dealing with difficult people and out-of-control circumstances, and the strain of making a living and a home. They also desired to know God and better understand what He wanted to do in their lives.

As the leader, you'll have the great privilege of shepherding group members in their discussions and in their commitments. You'll lead them through the study and guide them toward biblical answers to the circumstances of their lives. It is important that you prepare personally for each session both by reading the text and by praying for God to be present and active during the discussion time.

The body of each week's session contains—

For Openers — a contemporary setting to introduce a key theme from the woman's life and to help provide a modern-day angle on it.

Getting to Know Her — an overview of the main Scripture passage that will help put a real face on the Bible woman.

These first two sections should take about one-fourth of your total session time.

The Word Speaks—a time of reading and interacting with the key Scripture.

Where We Come In—a time of putting ourselves in the scene and making it our own.

These sections also contain sidebars—

- What Others Say
- Bible Background
- Did You Know?
- How It Works Today

Reading and discussing the questions in "The Word Speaks" and "Where We Come In" sections, along with the sidebar content, will make up the majority of your discussion.

However, just leaving your study at the theoretical stage is insufficient for real life change, so we've included a response section that you'll lead your group through. This is the pivotal moment of the study, where theory and insights translate into right-where-we-live actions. Try to spend about a quarter of your session time on these sections—

Responding through Prayer—where participants approach God and seek His guidance both individually and as a group. Group support is key, as accountability accompanies life change, and group dynamics come together in a special way as we approach God's throne together.

My Next Step—a practical, personal commitment toward life change for each participant.

Keep It in Mind—a simple, brief Bible verse that serves as a reminder throughout the week of the choices made in the session.

Take the first few moments of your time, beginning with your second session together, to ask how each participant applied the previous week's commitments. Encourage the group to feel free to share successes and struggles in this non-judgmental time. Holding one another accountable in this way will urge participants to follow through on the commitments they make each week.

I encourage you to do this shepherding prayerfully and with the grace and compassion that can flow only from your own personal relationship with Jesus Christ. At times the women of your group may need a listening ear, a compassionate challenge, or an act of kindness. At times you may need the same. But mostly you all will need a safe haven where you can learn together from God's Word, try and fail, and get up to try again. May your group become a place where God's presence is felt and where many women come to know Him in new and fresh ways.

When God does amazing things in your group, let us know about these victories. Let us share in the joy of His work in your life.

Contact us by writing to —

Wesleyan Publishing House
P.O. Box 50434
Indianapolis, IN 46250
Attn: Sisters in Faith

Or e-mail us at wph@wesleyan.org.

More Sisters in Faith Bible Studies

Courageous Women in the Bible
Step Out in Faith — Live Life with Purpose

Sisters in the Bible
Celebrate Relationships — Experience God's Power

Contents

Introduction   11

1. When God's Plan Doesn't Make Sense
    Jesus Transforms Us through Knowing Him   13

2. Healed and Valued by the Creator
    Jesus Transforms Our Faith—And Our Lives   21

3. An Unbelievable Turn of Events
    Jesus' Compassion Transforms Our Hurting Hearts   31

4. Love Is Unashamed
    Jesus Transforms Sinners into Saints   39

5. Tenacious Loyalty to the Master
    Transformation Results in Fruitful Ministry   47

6. A Most Unlikely Missionary
    Listening to Jesus Transforms Us   55

7. Caught and Released
    A True Glimpse of Jesus Transforms Our Own Self-Image   65

8. The Miracle of Christ's Compassion
    Worshipping God Brings Unexpected Transformation   73

Introduction

If I had to choose only one theme that would tie together all the divergent stories of women transformed by their encounters with Jesus as He walked this planet, it would be this: in a culture where women were despised at worst and ignored at best, Jesus valued women.

He entered the world as the Son of God through the seed of a woman. By doing this, He fulfilled His promise to the first woman that her offspring would crush the head of Satan, the tempter.

His interaction with the crowning glory of His creation didn't stop there. Jesus looked women in the eye when the religious leaders of the day looked away in superiority. He saw into their hearts and met their deepest needs. Jesus talked with them and listened when they talked to Him. He allowed (even invited) them to participate in learning alongside the disciples, in financially supporting His ministry, in standing beside Him when all others fled in fear, and in carrying the most exciting message of all—the news of His resurrection. Jesus treated women like valued sisters and like friends.

One would expect nothing less from the Creator who designed woman in His own image, forming her with His own hands and breathing into her His very own breath of life.

The Gospel writers record many examples of Jesus' personal and creative encounters with women during His ministry on earth. We will choose just a few of these encounters to examine in greater detail. We'll see how Jesus met these women's deepest needs, as they entrusted their care to the Creator who loved them and placed great eternal worth upon them.

As we come to understand their stories, we'll respond together to the challenge of bringing our own concerns to Jesus. And we will then watch as, amazingly, He transforms each of us.

1

When God's Plan Doesn't Make Sense

John 2:1–11; Mark 3:20–22, 31–35

*While Jesus was still talking to the crowd,
his mother and brothers stood outside,
wanting to speak to him.*

—Matthew 12:46

Discovery

Jesus transforms us through knowing Him.

For Openers

Have you ever marveled at the enthusiasm of a new believer in Christ? Have you observed her intoxicating spiritual high, her delight in breathing fresh heavenly air, and her freedom in soaring above life's problems on wings of joy? Now, be real here—if you've served Christ for more than a few years, you've probably sat by and thought cynically, just as I have, *This too shall pass.*

Too often I've let the routine of life chip away at the joy of my salvation and steal the wonder of knowing that the Creator of the universe values me. When time passes and His presence no longer seems so near, I usually get enmeshed in the battle of the day and lose sight of Him. If you've had a similar experience, you'll know that as our faith becomes dented, our assurance that He knows best is clouded by dashed expectations and misdirected hopes. After all, God's ways aren't our ways; neither is His timing in sequence with our schedule.

This is a truth we'll examine today in the life of a woman whom Christ dearly loved: His earthly mother, Mary. At some moments she shone with brilliant faith; at other times she was so mistaken that she actually attempted to derail the purposes of the Son of God. We're in good company if we've lost our way—but, like Mary, we don't need to stay mired in disappointment. We can again soar on the wings of renewed faith.

Getting to Know Her

More scenes focus on Mary, the mother of Jesus, than any other woman in the New Testament. She is named in at least ten events, spanning Jesus' entire earthly life. We often direct our attention to scenes listed early in the Gospels: Christ's annunciation by Gabriel, Mary visiting her cousin Elizabeth, or Mary giving birth to the Savior. These stories are worthy of study, but in the context of the transformation Jesus Christ brings to real women, we will focus today on scenes that take place later.

For example, as Jesus is growing into maturity in Luke 2:48–52, Mary tries to rebuke Him for staying behind in Jerusalem. There

He reminds her that He is about His Father's business—that He never has belonged to her and Joseph. Later, in Mark 3:31–35, she tries to interrupt Jesus' teachings when she perceives that they are ruffling more than a few Pharisaical feathers. There the Master bluntly rebuffs her efforts.

But Mary's story isn't *all* about misunderstanding. In John 2:1–11 we see Jesus, His disciples, and Mary at a wedding. She calls on Him to do something extraordinary to alleviate a friend's embarrassment, and He honors her request. Later, we see a grieving Mary, lovingly cared for by her eldest Son, as He is dying on the cross. At the end of her story, we see a rejoicing, believing Mary in one accord with the other followers, praying and awaiting the promised Holy Spirit. It is this believing Mary whose example we most want to emulate.

The Word Speaks

Have someone read **John 2:1–11**.

What can you surmise about the relationship between Son and mother in this scene? How is this different from the childhood scene described in Luke 2:48–52? What transition is Jesus making when He calls her "dear woman" rather than "mother" in John 2:4?

How does Mary's response show her respect for Jesus and her faith in Him? Note her authoritative tone in verse 5.

Now read **Mark 3:20-22, 31-35**.

Consider the context that the early verses in this passage provide, especially verse 21. How has Mary's perspective changed since the scene in Cana?

Perhaps Mary expected Jesus to overthrow the Romans and establish His rule on earth—restoring Israel to its former glory. Speculate on the notion that Mary was disappointed in her Son's unfolding ministry.

What Others Say

The context is important, for they came at the moment when opposition to Jesus was becoming open. It is also important to remember that long after this time "even his own brothers did not believe in him" (John 7:5). Why had the family delegation come? They had come to counsel this Son and Brother who was stirring up the countryside. They had come to try to calm Jesus—to urge Him to be less controversial!

—S. P. and L. Richards

Imagine growing up in the shadow of a *perfect* older brother, hearing often of His miraculous conception and His majestic purpose. Then observe how things appeared to be working out. Given the content of Jesus' message and the kinds of people pressing in on Him, how can you relate to the brothers' reaction?

Read the quote by S. P. and L. Richards. How does this perspective jibe with what you see in Scripture? How does it help you relate to the family's thoughts?

Why do you suppose the family stood outside and sent a messenger into the house to get Jesus? (Even if the crowd was pressing in, surely His family could have found a way into the inner circle.)

Jesus was in a difficult position; He was doing the will of His Father, knowing that His continued obedience had led both the religious leaders and His own family to conclude that He was deranged. Speculate on the contrast between His loyal disciples and His earthly family. How does this add to your understanding of Jesus' response in vv. 33–35? How does this indicate an understanding of His true purpose? Why do you think He refused to be interrupted, even to speak with His mother for a moment?

Read aloud John 19:25–27, then read the Bible Background note.

Though she didn't understand Him, Mary was there at Jesus' crucifixion, grieving, supporting, perhaps awaiting another miracle. What does this say about her faithfulness to Him? How does Jesus' tender care for Mary in this passage give perspective to the earlier scene when He elevated His followers to the place of family? How do Jesus' words in this passage demonstrate His love for her?

Bible Background

The Bible's plan for families is a fairly straightforward one: Parents care for children until they reach adulthood; then children have a responsibility for the care of their parents. This was considered an integral part of "honoring" mothers and fathers, as commanded by the Law (Exodus 20:12).

—*Woman's Study Bible*

Where We Come In

Think back to the Cana wedding. When have you, like Mary, demonstrated an unwavering faith in Jesus? How has He proven himself faithful? What effect does this kind of faith have on those around you? (Reread John 2:11.) How has your faith grown as a result?

Putting yourself in the place of Mary, when have you misunderstood what God was doing in your life? How about in your children's lives? Name a time when you put up roadblocks to interrupt His work in you or your family because you didn't like the direction He was taking you. What was the result? How do you wish you would have responded?

How It Works Today

Janet Grippo and her husband, Joe, have spent countless hours praying for their three children and nine grandchildren.

Their son Paul is a cancer research doctor. Over the years Janet has prayed these prayers for him: "Give him a dream from God to pursue. Allow him to find favor with God and his professors. Give him success in working toward a cure for pancreatic cancer. Keep him faithful to his calling and to God."

Janet says, "In some instances it took miracles to bring Paul through. At times it looked bleak, but we kept praying and believing that God would make a way for him if this was what He had planned for Paul."

Janet's prayer list lacks any overtone of a parent trying to control a child's decisions or trying to exert her own wishes upon him. Instead, she asks God to provide direction, goals, insights, and vision to each member of her family, Paul included.

Read Janet Grippo's story. How do Janet's prayers and dreams for her son and family differ from what we read about Jesus' family? What actions can you take to show that you're on board with what God wants to do in your loved ones' lives?

In Acts 1:12–14, Mary comes full circle. As a teenage virgin she exhibited great faith, in her middle years she didn't understand her holy Son, but in the end she became an obedient follower and redeemed one. What progression have you seen in your faith over time?

We're in good company when we waver from the heights of faith to the depths of doubt. Think of Mary, whom the angel Gabriel called "highly favored" (Luke 1:28), and think of Peter and his bold recognition of Jesus as the Messiah (Matt. 16:16) and his cowardly denial of Jesus before a servant girl (Matt. 26:69–70). Then see both of them (with Jesus' formerly unbelieving brothers) in Acts 1 exhibiting faith in and obedience to their Savior. Where are you in your faith journey? Where would you like to be? What can you draw from Mary's example to help you get to a new place of faith?

Read the note from the *Believer's Bible Commentary*. How did Mary become a part of Jesus' spiritual family? How can we join Jesus' spiritual family? What role does obedience to Him play in joining? Since Jesus' spiritual

> ### Did You Know?
>
> [Jesus] recognizes as members of His family all who tremble at the word, who receive it with meekness, and who obey it implicitly. No crowd can prevent His spiritual family from having audience with Him.
>
> —*Believer's Bible Commentary*

family members have unlimited access to His throne room, carry your needs to Him today.

Responding through Prayer

Pray silently, allowing God's Spirit to speak to your heart through what you've read. Then, speak sentence-prayers expressing your belief in Jesus, obedience in carrying out God's plan for your life, and entrusting your loved ones into His all-wise care. Encourage each of your fellow participants to share one prayer in each category.

My Next Step

To help me know Jesus better, this week I will:

Keep It in Mind

The book of James is attributed to the half-brother of Jesus. He may not have believed early on, but clearly he came around. Keep these words of his in mind this week: "Do not merely listen to the word, and so deceive yourselves. Do what it says" (James 1:22).

2

Healed and Valued By the Creator

Mark 5:21–43

When she heard about Jesus, she came up behind him in the crowd and touched his cloak, because she thought, "If I just touch his clothes, I will be healed."

—Mark 5:27–28

Discovery

Jesus transforms our faith—and our lives.

For Openers

Crowds. They give me the willies. I'm not afraid of them, but I am uncomfortable in them. A product of twentieth-century western culture, I am fiercely protective of my individuality, my uniqueness, and my personal space.

My first job took me from a spacious suburban comfort zone right into the center of Chicago's jam-packed loop. I never became accustomed to disembarking a passenger train every morning into a moving mass of humanity, elbowing my way across the bridge and up the streets of the business district. After two and a half years, I seized an opportunity to return to a self-directed life in the burbs without a backward glance.

But there is something to be said for crowds. When we're trying to keep from being noticed or identified, joining the crowd may be the way to go. That's what the woman whom we'll be focusing on today was hoping. The crushing crowd pressed in on Jesus and provided just the opportunity she needed to anonymously get her healing and get out before the Teacher knew she was there. Or so she hoped.

As we walk in her sandals, we'll see that in God's eyes, none of us is just a face in the crowd. As He knew her and kept an appointment with her, so He knows each of us—tearing away our anonymity, replacing it with treasured personhood.

Getting to Know Her

She has a plan. Ill-advised, perhaps. Desperate even. But filled with faith. Although every other effort she has made has been in vain, this plan has a chance.

She's heard about a healer, and He is expected to pass her way. Since He is a religious man (she knows how repulsed by her disease the religious are), she has to be clandestine. Sneak up behind Him. Touch the outer fringes of His robe as it swishes through the sandy street. He won't notice, therefore she won't make Him unclean by touching Him. But maybe, just maybe, that touch will be sufficient to free her from the sickening hemorrhage she's endured these twelve years. In this simple plan she places all her remaining hope.

Her heart pounds in her ears. Her already-weakened legs turn to jelly as Jesus approaches. She chooses her station where the procession will pass. Jesus is hurrying by with Jairus, the synagogue leader. The crowds are fierce. But that is good, because she'll be all the more invisible. Her arm darts out. Her fingers barely brush the tassel they had been seeking. In less than an instant, she feels the bleeding cease. Unbelievable strength returns to her. She shrinks back, leaping for joy on the inside, but unable to let any exuberance show on the outside.

Just then, the Teacher stops, eyes searching the crowd, and asks, "Who touched me?" Her joy morphs into abject panic. *He can't know! How could He? He'll take it back, and I'll never be free.* She clings to her anonymity as long as she can. But finally—perhaps His eyes lock with hers—she flings herself at the feet of the Teacher, confessing all, and waiting in silence to learn the price she must pay for her impertinence.

The Word Speaks

Silently read **Mark 5:21-43**, listening for what God has to say to you.

In this text we have a story within a story. Let's begin with the outer story, that of the synagogue ruler Jairus and his desperate move to save his dying daughter. What kind of faith must it have taken for Jairus to fall at Jesus' feet and plead for his daughter's life? What opposition might he have met from his peers? How does his valuing of his daughter provide an apt setting for what happens next?

Matthew says Jesus was teaching the crowd when Jairus approached. Yet Jesus didn't seem to mind the interruption. Mark explains, "So Jesus went with him." What does this tell you about how Jesus values individuals? Do you suppose Jesus was willing to go with Jairus because he was a powerful man, or was it Jairus' heartfelt plea that moved Jesus? What makes you think so?

Bible Background

Her disorder was of that delicate nature that modesty forbade her to make any public acknowledgment of it; and therefore she endeavored to transact the whole business in private. Besides, the touch of such a person was by the law reputed unclean.

—Adam Clarke

Now we encounter the interruption of the suffering woman. Read the quote from Adam Clarke. How much faith did it take for this woman to approach Jesus?

Read the quote from Archibald Thomas Robertson. Given the crushing nature of the crowd, it wouldn't have been easy to get close enough to touch the fringe of Jesus' cloak. How do you connect with the desperation of placing the last shred of hope on such a long shot?

Reread verses 30–34, this time aloud. Why do you think Jesus took time to stop? He had allowed her to be healed immediately. What more could He have wanted from her? Or *for* her?

> **Did You Know?**
>
> *The border of his garment* is the hem or fringe of a garment, a tassel or tuft hanging from the edge of the outer garment according to Numbers 15:38. It was made of twisted wool. Jesus wore the dress of other people with these fringes at the four corners of the outer garment.
>
> —Archibald Thomas Robertson

Feel the frustration of Jairus at this interruption, when every moment was as crucial as the next. Feel the consternation of the disciples, who might have thought to themselves, *Who knows and who cares? Heal the little girl, and get us all on the good side of the rulers.* Feel the panic of the woman. Then feel the unspeakable love of the Master. Which emotion supercedes all the others? Why?

Why did Jesus take the woman's anonymity away? What did He give her in return? How much more valuable was His gift than the initial physical healing?

Jairus' daughter died, possibly during this exchange. But Jesus' plan wasn't interrupted, even by death. He and His inner circle continued on to Jairus' house, where Jesus brought the girl back to life. What lessons might Jesus have been teaching Jairus' family and His disciples?

Where We Come In

When do you suppose Jesus first became aware of the woman—when He felt the power go out from Him, or sometime before that? Why do you suppose He allowed himself to be interrupted by her *spiritual* need? What spiritual need do you have today?

Think back to Jesus' refusal to be interrupted by His mother and brothers in Mark 3:31–34. Contrast His response in that situation with His response to the interruptions in Mark 5. What can you learn from these two scenes about discerning between God-ordained interruptions and derailing interruptions? What does Jesus' example teach you about how to respond in each case? Has your life ever been interrupted by God? Tell about that time.

What Others Say

Her fear of illness and death was surpassed by her awe at this one who knew He had healed her . . . Jesus' address "Daughter" brought her into relationship with Him based on her saving faith (5:34). This new relationship makes going in God's peace possible.

—Christopher L. Church

Discuss the quote from Christopher Church. What role does faith play in the woman's healing? How would you define faith? (See Hebrews 11:1 for a hint.)

Read Hebrews 11:6. According to this verse, why does it matter where you place your faith?

How It Works Today

Evelyn Christenson and her husband Chris intended to spend their lives in India carrying the gospel. Chris, a pilot in World War II, was planning to be a flying evangelist. However, when he returned from the war with a bleeding ulcer, the doctor would not clear the couple to minister overseas—a major interruption in their life plans. Disappointed, they entered the pastorate in the United States.

While Chris pastored, Evelyn undertook a prayer experiment with the women of their congregation. This experiment became the impetus for her internationally best-selling book, *What Happens When Women Pray,* and a large number of related books and products—not to mention countless answered prayers. This phenomenon catapulted Evelyn into an international writing and speaking ministry, which thirty years later (to the month) brought her to India with a huge supply of books and teaching tapes. She says, "God knew what He was doing. Had I gone to India in 1952, I would not have done anything but be the navigator in Chris's airplane."

What situations have called for you to act in faith? How has God proven himself worthy?

Read the story about Evelyn Christenson. Discuss the godly dream she had, the disappointment of being denied that path, and the eventual fulfillment of a much better dream. Does having faith always mean you immediately get what you want from God? Why not? (Think of how Jairus must have been feeling after learning that Jesus' delay had cost his daughter her life.)

How is the phrase "God is good" still true when life doesn't work out as you plan? In what instances have you learned to trust God, though he did not say, "Yes," to your earnest requests?

Read Jesus' compassionate words to the woman in Mark 5:34 aloud, as a group. Silently let those words sink into your heart, as though Jesus is speaking them to you.

Responding through Prayer

Make this your heart's prayer: *God, I want to have faith like this anonymous woman. I, too, need to be healed—physically, emotionally, and spiritually—and loved and valued by You. Let me hear You call me Daughter. Please grant me Your lasting peace, and Your gift of freedom from suffering. I will be forever grateful.*

My Next Step

Each day this week I will approach God in Jesus' name asking Him to do in these areas of my life what no one else can do:

Keep It in Mind

Just as Jesus honored the woman's faith, so He also desires to honor our faith. This week, commit this Scripture to memory: "And without faith it is impossible to please God, because anyone who comes to him must believe that he exists and that he rewards those who earnestly seek him" (Heb. 11:6).

3

An Unbelievable Turn Of Events

Luke 7:11–23

As he approached the town gate, a dead person was being carried out—the only son of his mother, and she was a widow. And a large crowd from the town was with her. When the Lord saw her, his heart went out to her and he said, "Don't cry."

—Luke 7:12–13

Discovery

Jesus' compassion transforms our hurting hearts.

For Openers

When I was a magazine editor, we received an article from a freelance writer who wrote for us often. I can't recall other subjects she tackled for us, but I can recall this article, "Please Just Tell Me You're Sorry." The subject was her multiple miscarriages, and, in particular, how people in her circle of friends (even her church) didn't know what to say to her afterward.

She said there was nothing anyone could say that would bring her babies back. But friends could have provided a shoulder to cry on and the heartfelt words: "Go ahead and cry; I'm so sorry you have to face this." It may be downright frustrating, but sometimes that is all we can do when we encounter a fellow sufferer: come alongside the mourning one and let her know we care.

Not so with the Son of God, though. His human heart goes out to the sufferer, as we'll see today. But His compassion has hands and legs; His words have the power of life over death. The amazing thing is that He marshals these resources on behalf of a widow woman in a seemingly chance encounter.

Getting to Know Her

Without even being in the same building, Jesus has just accomplished the healing of a centurion's servant (Luke 7:1–10). It is a magnificent testimony to foreigners and Jews. Then, He and His growing band of followers are on the move. They are heading toward the city of Nain; but only Jesus knows why. (Read the "Did You Know?" note to learn about this location.)

The road into Nain is the same road those from the city had to travel to reach the place where they bury their dead (always outside the city proper). At the exact moment when Jesus' procession approaches the city, a

> ## Did You Know?
>
> Nain was about eight kilometers (five miles) southeast of Nazareth on the northern edge of the Plain of Esdraelon. The present-day Arab village of Nein covers ruins of a much larger town.
>
> —*Nelson's New Illustrated Bible Dictionary*

boisterous procession is carrying the lifeless body of a man, the only son of a widow woman, to the burial grounds.

Jesus and His procession meet the mourners head-on. But the mother, in her grief, doesn't look up until Jesus stops both processions and addresses her, "Don't cry." Can you imagine her disdain? *What business do you have telling me not to cry? I'll cry if I want to. My only son is gone forever.*

There are a few constants in this world. One of those constants is that dead men don't sit up and talk. It just doesn't happen. Dead men don't do anything at all, except lie there. But when Jesus enters the picture, He turns everything upside down. Death gives way to life. Sorrow gives way to inexpressible joy. Old ways of life vanish to make room for newness previously unknown.

The funny thing about these changes: we don't expect them. We're going along, like the widowed mother—weeping, wailing, mourning—so enmeshed in circumstances that we don't see Jesus walk up to the casket of our smashed dreams and speak words of vibrant new life.

The Word Speaks

Have three volunteers read **Luke 7:11-23** from the same translation. Ask one to read the narration, the second to read the words spoken by Jesus, and the third to read the quotes from the crowd and the followers of John.

Consider the context—the placement of this story between the healing of the centurion's servant and the questioning of Jesus. How does the progression from one scene to the next influence your reading of the raising of the woman's son?

Jesus spoke a simple command, "Young man, I say to you, get up!" Then, the man not only gets up, but he also begins talking. Don't you wish you could have heard his first words? What would you have asked him?

Bible Background

Up from the city close by came this "great multitude" that followed the dead, with lamentations, wild chaunts of mourning women, accompanied by flutes and the melancholy tinkle of cymbals, perhaps by trumpets, amidst expressions of general sympathy. Along the road from Endor streamed the great multitude which followed the "Prince of Life." Here they met: Life and Death. The connecting link between them was the deep sorrow of the widowed mother.

—Alfred Edersheim

This was one of several recorded encounters Jesus had with death and resurrection. The story of Jairus' daughter (Mark 5) is another example, as is the story of Lazarus (John 11). Scan both of these passages. What new information does each add to your understanding of Jesus' power over the scourge of sin and death?

Read the quote from Alfred Edersheim. Consider the statement "Here they met: Life and Death." Give your thoughts on this curious meeting of opposites on the road to Nain. Why is it crucial to know that God's Son is Lord even over the great equalizer, death?

We don't have a response from the mother, as Jesus gave her son back to her. (Perhaps she was speechless.) We do know that the crowd was profoundly affected. Note their responses (7:16–17). If your only knowledge and interaction with Jesus were from this scene in the Bible, what conclusions would you have drawn about Him? Whom would you have told about Him?

As you consider reasons Jesus might have chosen to raise this man in such a public setting, look at the ripple of impact it had. Not only did word spread among the common people of Galilee, but it reached all the way to John the Baptist, who was languishing in a Judean prison. Why do you suppose Jesus responded as He did to the disciples John sent (7:18–23)? What was His underlying message to John?

What Others Say

With infinite love and compassion our Lord understood the human predicament. He had deep empathy with people; He saw their needs, their weaknesses, their desires, and their hurts. He understood and was concerned for people. Every word He spoke was uttered because He saw a need for that word in some human life.

—Charles L. Allen

Where We Come In

Read the quote by Charles L. Allen. How do you see Jesus' understanding of your "human predicament" in this story? How is this consistent with how you've seen Jesus work in your life and in the lives of those around you?

Share with the group some ways you have felt this same sense of understanding from Jesus in your life.

There would have been a great wailing sound accompanying the funeral procession—much of it from paid mourners. How comforting do you suppose those mourners were for the woman who had lost not only her beloved son, but also her only source of care and protection? When have people tried to offer you this kind of comfort?

When you are comforting someone, what can you do to be of genuine help? If you have suffered grief, share with the group some tangible ways others have helped you.

How It Works Today

Marilyn and Bill Berg are parents of an adult son who died of AIDS. Their son Al made lifestyle choices that disappointed his parents, and he suffered dire consequences. But rather than being judgmental, they cuddled and nursed and served him until his dying day—making it a priority to see that Al made peace with God before passing into eternity. Recalling how she felt as her son withered before her eyes, Marilyn said she'd never get over losing her son to this ruthless disease.

But what is truly amazing about Marilyn and Bill is what they did after Al died: they funneled their grief into helping other victims. After taking classes at a hospice, they volunteered to serve others dying of AIDS.

Yes, they grieved. But they didn't wallow. They acted in compassion to share Christ's touchable love with others whose time to decide to follow Jesus was painfully short.

Read Hebrews 4:13–16. Listen to the progression: first, a reminder that God knows everything, then a reminder of Jesus' empathy, and, finally, a challenge to keep faith grounded in Him and to carry burdens to Him. Which of these reminders resonates most with you this week? Are you in need of His all-knowing nature? His compassionate embrace? Or His strong arms to carry your burden? Why?

Note that Jesus acted on behalf of this woman, even though she hadn't asked Him to do so. Describe a time when you were so overwhelmed that you couldn't even form the words to pray. How did you feel God come alongside you, even when you were too weak to ask? What did His presence do to bolster your spirits and your faith? How did friends help you?

To this point, we've focused on what Jesus and other people can do for those who sorrow. But there is often something we can do to help ourselves when mourning. Read the story in the sidebar. How did the actions of these grieving parents contribute to their healing? If you are going through a difficult time, in what tangible ways can you reach out to others? How might this affect your burden?

Responding through Prayer

Jesus, I know You see my situation today, just as You saw all the widow of Nain needed. I place my trust in You completely because I know You understand my weaknesses and feel my pain. I am comforted by that. So I look into Your eyes and I ask You to take control of my areas of need.

My Next Step

Think of someone in your circle of friends, family, or acquaintances who has lost all hope. Prayerfully ask Jesus to meet that person's deepest needs; then ask Him how you can be part of the answer. Do whatever He shows you to do:

-

-

Keep It in Mind

As you go into your week, keep the picture of Christ's compassion near to your heart. Knowing this, make the following Scripture your own: "Let us then approach the throne of grace with confidence, so that we may receive mercy and find grace to help us in our time of need" (Heb. 4:16).

4

Love Is Unashamed

Luke 7:36–50

*Jesus said to the woman,
"Your faith has saved you; go in peace."*

—Luke 7:50

Discovery

Jesus transforms sinners into saints.

For Openers

The other night, a Food Network chef was making chili and wanted to speed up the cooking time. He got out a pressure cooker, poured in the ingredients, clamped the lid on tightly, and cranked up the heat. When the cooking was over, he couldn't simply take the lid off by the handle; he had to push a release valve. That release caused a caustic hissing and forced out volumes of steam. Instinctively, the chef jerked away. Only after all the steam was released could he open the lid and get at the delicious contents.

Although I didn't pay much attention in applied sciences classes, I did pick up enough knowledge to remember that trapped steam builds up enough pressure to cook a stew, turn an electricity-generating turbine, or explode if not contained properly.

The building pressure and volatility of steam is a great illustration of the situation we'll encounter today. Guilt and sin had built up inside the woman we'll meet, to the point of combustion. Clamped on and jammed down, the pressure grew increasingly intense over multiple years. But when Jesus' words offered a release valve—the forgiveness of sin—the steam billowed out in volumes of love and gratefulness that simply couldn't be contained. From her example, we'll gain a new appreciation of the value of being clean before God—and of being truly thankful for that priceless gift.

Getting to Know Her

She is known as a sinner; her fame in town is unmistakable. She has lived up to her reputation, in a very public way. But then she begins hearing snatches of conversations about a teacher, perhaps a prophet, headed into town. No one knows what to make of Him. But something quickens in her spirit. Something drives her to find this Teacher—and perhaps catch a few words of His intriguing message.

When He makes His way into town, she listens. Her heart is touched, and she finds herself repenting of her sin. Perhaps she hears the Teacher's words, "Come to me, all you who are weary and burdened, and I will give you rest . . . For my yoke is easy and my burden is light" (Matt. 11:28–30). Whether it was these or other soothing words of forgiveness, we don't know. But we do know that when she comes to Jesus, gratefulness multiplies inside her, building up into deep love for her new Master, until it is more than one woman's heart could possibly contain.

Jesus is dining as the invited guest of a religious leader. But that doesn't stop her. She makes her way into the hall of celebration and cuts a path directly to Him. She breaks open her flask of oil and begins to weep. Her tears mingle with the oil and wash His feet. Perhaps embarrassed, she wipes His wet feet with her long tresses.

He then looks at her, directly in the eye. She knows He knows. And she knows she is truly forgiven. The other men attending the banquet are saying things about her, but she ignores them. Their shock and indignation are nothing to her. They have always been shocked and indignant about her behavior—unless, perchance, they had been benefiting from it. But the response of Jesus—that is new to her. Refreshing. Welcomed. Deliciously freeing.

The Word Speaks

Read aloud **Luke 7:36-50**. Listen both for what Jesus *did* say and what He *didn't* say. Pay special attention to His skillful handling of an awkward mix of people and unfolding events.

Share your thoughts on the way Jesus conducted himself in the Pharisee's home. How was His conduct creatively gracious toward

Did You Know?

In New Testament times it was common for a woman to wear a vial of perfumed oil around her neck. Often it was used to mask unpleasant odors, moisturize the skin in the arid climate, or provide a symbol of honor when poured over the head or feet of invited guests.

—*Woman's Study Bible*

Simon? Toward the woman? How did He keep from embarrassing the host while not compromising His message?

Read the note from the *Woman's Study Bible*. How does this detail help your understanding of the situation? Why did Luke make a point of recording how expensive this perfumed oil was? Why might the woman have been carrying it? Do you think her opening the flask and pouring it on Jesus' feet was a premeditated act (as in, she went home to get it) or an act of unbridled enthusiasm? Was it worth the expenditure?

Read the "Bible Background" note. Edersheim adds context when he notes that while it wasn't absolutely necessary for Simon to perform acts of service toward his guest, it would have been a sign of respect and honor. How, then, does this woman's act contrast with Simon's lack of action?

Bible Background

To wash the feet of a guest, to give him the kiss of welcome, and especially to anoint him, were not, indeed, necessary attentions at a feast. All the more did they indicate special care, affection, and respect. None of these tokens of deep regard had marked the merely polite reception of Him by the Pharisee.

—Alfred Edersheim

Do you think Luke purposely chose not to name this woman? How could anonymity have benefited the woman at a later time? Given the whole of the story, does it appear that she chose to follow Jesus and leave her life of sin?

What Others Say

There is humility and devotion in the woman's act of service, as well as a great deal of courage, as she performed the deed in front of a crowd that knew her as a sinner. Although the woman does not say a word in the entire account, her actions speak volumes about her contrite heart.

—*Nelson's New Illustrated Bible Commentary*

Read the note from *Nelson's Commentary*. Then discuss the courage the woman needed to approach Jesus in this semi-public setting. What would make it possible (or necessary) for her to break through the cultural norms and minister to Jesus in such a hands-on way? In what ways does Jesus indicate that He not only allows this service, but welcomes it?

What or who in your life makes you hesitant to run freely to Jesus to offer your love, worship, and service? How can this woman's example make you bolder and less concerned about what others think?

Where We Come In

Why do you suppose Jesus chose to confront Simon's judgmental thoughts with a story rather than a direct accusation? What do you learn from the story Jesus tells in verses 41–43? What comfort do you find in knowing that Jesus knew Simon's thoughts—and the woman's sincere heart?

In Jewish thought of that day, Simon's conclusion in verse 43 would have been a typical one; he assumed that the woman's sins were much greater than his own. Was that truly the case in Jesus' eyes? What danger is there in comparing our sins with those of others? How does self-righteousness get in the way of acknowledging our sins to God? How does it short-circuit our gratefulness?

How It Works Today

Rose Malavolti is a godly woman who loves much. Rose decided as a grade-schooler that she wanted twenty-one children, by birth and adoption. In adulthood she and her husband Al had four birth children and took in dozens of foster children—a busy household by any definition. But the adoption dream wouldn't die.

Eventually, they met Blanca, an illegal immigrant in Texas, who was dying of cancer. Blanca's wish was that her eight minor-aged children (ages nineteen months to seventeen years) be kept together. Rose and Al prayerfully added these new members to their family with one stroke of the pen.

They couldn't have anticipated the changes—from overtaxing their home's plumbing system, to astronomical costs of feeding the clan, to Rose homeschooling the children to make up for educational deficiencies. Even their kitchen table needed to be exchanged for a twenty-foot custom-crafted model that allowed mealtime seating for the family of fourteen.

The key to their household's success? According to Rose, it's love. Amid the thirty-four loads of laundry each week, Rose gives and receives more hugs than she can count—and she counts herself truly blessed.

In light of this conversation, have you been forgiven little or much? How much do you love the Master? How do you show that love through acts of service toward Him and His body?

Read the story of Rose Malavolti. How is Rose putting into practice her deep love for Jesus Christ? What is that love in action costing her? What does it mean to the eight children she and Al took into their hearts and their home? What does it mean to their four birth children? What do you suppose those children are learning from their parents' example? What do you glean from Rose's example?

Turn to 2 Corinthians 12:7–10. Pay special attention to v. 9, then read the quote from Anne Ortlund. Anne shows us a picture of God just waiting to rush to us with forgiveness if we'll only come to Him in faith. How is this picture consistent with the way Jesus interacted with the woman in today's story? How is it consistent with the forgiveness He offers you? What does this knowledge motivate you to do right now?

> ### What Others Say
>
> How could [Paul] "boast gladly about his weaknesses"? Because he understood how gladly God forgives! He knew that when we rush to God with our confessions, God rushes to us with His forgiveness.
>
> —Anne Ortlund

Responding through Prayer

Come to God in silence with the question: *In light of the forgiveness You have offered me, how can I love You more?* Listen quietly until His answer is clear. After several minutes, close with words like these: *Father, each of us is grateful for the gifts You have lavished on us. Help us this week, to lavish our love and gratitude on You and on those who come across our paths.*

My Next Step

With a lack of concern for what others are thinking, I will _____ this week, purely motivated out of my love for Christ and my gratitude to Him.

Other steps I'll take:

-
-

Keep It in Mind

Each day this week, meditate on 1 John 4:12, and put it into practice: "No one has ever seen God; but if we love one another, God lives in us and his love is made complete in us."

5

Tenacious Loyalty To the Master

Luke 8:1–3; 23:49–24:11

*After this, Jesus traveled about from one town
and village to another, proclaiming the good news of
the kingdom of God. The Twelve were with him, and
also some women who had been cured of evil
spirits and diseases. . . . These women were helping
to support them out of their own means.*

—Luke 8:1–3

Discovery

Transformation results in fruitful ministry.

For Openers

Rumors. They can be cruel and hurtful. Seldom will someone start a rumor with a pure motive. Most often they emerge out of jealousy, vindictiveness, or even pure hatred. They are designed to discredit, to cast aspersions, to tear someone down. The worst rumors are those tinged with a tiny morsel of truth. The mingling of truth and falsehood makes these the most difficult to disprove, especially when right and wrong become clouded.

Ultimately, rumors bruise the truth—dent it a little in some people's minds. But rumors can't obscure the truth from the knowledge of true seekers.

Rumors will play a role in the lives of the women we'll meet in the Word today. There were rumors about them then, rumors about them in the early church age, and rumors about them even today in popular twenty-first-century fiction. But for those of us who seek genuine knowledge from the pages of Scripture, we'll find that the truth about their lives and relationships with Jesus is much more powerful than any rumor. We'll discover the secrets of these remarkable women, who were known by their Master as trustworthy, generous, and courageous. And, most of all, we'll learn from their example to make the most of the gifts He gives us to serve Him and His body.

Getting to Know Her (and Her and Her)

In an era in which female students outnumber males on many college campuses, it may be difficult for us to imagine just how *avant-garde* it was for Jesus, in His day, to teach, touch, heal, and publicly accept financial support from women. But He freely offers deliverance and salvation from bondage to all who come to Him—men and women—accepting their varying degrees of devotion.

The women named in Luke 8:1–3 are three of the many who followed Jesus. They would have been well-known in the church at the time of Luke's writing (approximately A.D. 58), which may explain why the three are named.

In today's passage we meet Mary Magdalene (whose story inter-sects with Jesus' when she is delivered from seven demons that tormented her). We also meet Joanna (whose husband was wealthy and powerful in Herod's court), and Susanna. Each of these women has access to her own wealth (or at least has her hus-band's support in giving financially to Jesus' ministry). Each has been delivered from much suffering, torment, or illness by Jesus. And each is more grateful than mere words could express.

Not only do these women give financially, but they are privileged to travel alongside Jesus and His disciples. They observe the mir-acles, hear the parables, listen to the teaching, and get to know their Savior by spending time with Him every day. Hardships must be many for women on this journey, as even the Lord him-self doesn't always have a place to lay His head (Luke 9:58). But still they follow. Still they give. Until the end—or is it the begin-ning? For their dedication and service is rewarded with the ulti-mate privilege, that of witnessing the Savior's death and then bearing the incomprehensible news of His resurrection.

The Word Speaks

Have one person from the group read aloud **Luke 8:1-3**. Then have two other volunteers alternate reading paragraphs from **Luke 23:49-24:11**.

List all of the sacrifices Joanna, Susanna, Mary Magdalene, and the other women might have had to make to camp with the crowds following Jesus from town to town. Why did these three wealthy women, in particular, set aside their lives of privilege to listen to Jesus every day?

How do the details Luke provides in 8:1–3 help you understand the women's circumstances before and after encountering Jesus? How can you relate to the way they expressed their gratitude in tangible, costly ways?

Did You Know?

Magdala was a wealthy city known in Jesus' time for manufacturing dye and woolen textiles, and for providing large quantities [of] turtle doves and pigeons to the temple in Jerusalem for use as purification offerings.

—Alfred Edersheim

Read the information about Magdala. How do these details about the city where Mary made her home give insight into her background?

Turn your attention to Jesus' death and burial (Luke 23). Why do you suppose Luke included the phrase "including the women who had followed him from Galilee" (Luke 23:49) in his telling? Contrast the presence of these women at Jesus' crucifixion with the absence of the crowds of people that had pressed in so many other times to see miracles and eat free food. What does this tell you about the women's dedication? What does it tell you about their courage in being willing to publicly associate with Jesus when the Roman government and Jewish leaders considered Him a condemned criminal?

As you reread Luke 23:49–56, imagine it as a scene from a mystery movie when the hero tails a suspect in hopes of gaining information. Feel the heart-pounding intensity as the hero watches and follows. Translate that feeling into the scene as the women follow Joseph of Arimathea to Pilate's palace and then the tomb. How does this help you gain a new appreciation for these women?

Alfred Edersheim describes Mary Magdalene "as prominent among the pious women as Peter was among the Apostles." Mary was prominent in the announcement of the resurrection; she was the first to see Jesus alive. Read John 20:14–18. Discuss why this was such a privilege. Suggest reasons God might have chosen this woman to carry *this* message. What does this choice tell you about the rewards of heartfelt service to the Lord?

Where We Come In

Read the "What Others Say" note. How have these rumors about Mary Magdalene affected how you have thought about her? When have rumors impacted your life? How have you tried (successfully or unsuccessfully) to combat them? How have they changed your actions or attitudes? What does your own experience tell you about believing or spreading rumors?

What Others Say

There is an almost indestructible body of myth that has come to surround [Mary Magdalene], primarily by reason of speakers, writers, novelists, and screen-plays, which have created a fantasy that generally suggests three things, *none* of which are in the Bible: (1) that she had been a prostitute, (2) that she was young and attractive, and (3) that she had a romantic affection for Jesus.

—Jack Hayford

Bible Background

First, she was a grateful soul, because she had been freed from terrible torment. This text suggests her service for Christ was motivated by that gratitude. Second, she was a witness of the Crucifixion . . . (The fact that the other women with whom she kept company were all older women supports the reasoning that she was likely their peer in age.) Third, she was present at Jesus' burial . . . and the first person actually to talk with Jesus after He was risen.

—Jack Hayford

Read Jack Hayford's explanation of the truth about Mary. What truths in Scripture debunk the rumors that have followed her? Why does her character and motivation matter?

What traits of Mary, Joanna, and Susanna can you translate into your life? How does their example of generosity with their resources and themselves provide an indictment to you? What does it challenge you to do?

What have you given up to follow Jesus? Has it been worth the sacrifice? Is He asking you to give Him more than you are willing to offer?

From what old ways of life has Jesus set you free? How are you expressing your gratitude and dedication to Him? How can you be more diligent in this area?

In Luke 24:6 the angels tell the women, "Remember how he told you, while he was still with you in Galilee . . ." Why do you suppose the women needed to be reminded of what they had heard Jesus say? What reminders do you need when crisis or sorrow obscures Jesus' promises to you? What reminders do you need of His love for you, His purpose for your life, His promise to be with you until the end of the age (Matt. 28:20)?

Compare Jesus' instructions to Mary (John 20:17) and those given by the angels with the words of the resurrected Savior in Matthew 28:18–20. How does the Great Commission to carry the good news of His sacrifice and resurrection apply to you today?

How It Works Today

Pam Myers is a suburban soccer mom who prayed that her daughter Natalie, then in second grade, would have "a nice little girlfriend" in school. As if in answer to the prayer, Natalie began playing with Anna. Over the summer, Natalie invited Anna to her church's vacation Bible school, and Pam became friends with Anna's mother, Antigone.

Antigone confided in Pam that she was raised Greek Orthodox, but her husband wasn't. She said they had decided to find a church to attend together.

Pam prayed. Then when all the parents were invited to the church for a VBS closing dinner, Antigone and her husband, Nick, came. Two weeks later they began attending the church on Sundays. Late in the summer, Antigone accepted Christ; her husband followed that fall. Pam discipled Antigone in the faith; Pam's husband discipled Nick. And Natalie was turned on to evangelism for life.

Reflecting on the story about Pam Myers, identify at least one friend or family member who needs to hear about Jesus. Discuss with your group creative ways you might introduce your loved ones to the Savior.

Responding through Prayer

Bow your head for prayer. Then have each member of your group take turns speaking sentence-prayers: prayers of gratefulness, then prayers of personal dedication, and finally prayers for direction in carrying out the gospel's challenge.

My Next Step

Thinking back on my loved one who needs to hear about Jesus, I commit to take the following steps toward sharing the good news with that person this week:

■

■

Keep It in Mind

Make this verse your goal in the coming week: "Your beauty . . . should be that of your inner self, the unfading beauty of a gentle and quiet spirit, which is of great worth in God's sight" (1 Pet. 3:3–4).

6

A Most Unlikely Missionary

John 4:4–30, 39–42

*Then, leaving her water jar, the woman went back
to the town and said to the people, "Come, see a
man who told me everything I ever did.
Could this be the Christ?"*

—John 4:28–29

Discovery

Listening to Jesus transforms us.

For Openers

What a terrible legacy the current worship wars in the
church will leave to future generations. The body of
Christ is crippled and divided by a fruitless debate about whether
God is more pleased with guitars and drums, or pianos and
organs; with long-meandering melodies, or simple tunes of the
people; with short ditties that keep replaying in your head, or
meaty lyrics that leave you pondering for days. Somehow, I doubt

that God is pleased with anything offered in the name of worship that has as its foundation the competition or superiority of one human-focused method over another.

As Jesus explained to the woman we'll meet today, the worship His Father seeks isn't about method or tied to a location. Rather, He seeks worship that focuses on Him, from hearts that adore Him and forget themselves entirely in the process. This powerful pronouncement should resound in our churches—and put an end to the debate once and for all. If we heed this direction, not only our churches, but our very lives, will be renewed in ways we can't begin to imagine.

Getting to Know Her

She is going about her business on a most ordinary day. She decides to draw water from the far-away Jacob's well, rather than the nearby town well, to avoid the snubs and sideways glances of the gossips. As she lowers her bucket into the ancient well, she hears a voice behind her—an unfamiliar male voice with a Galilean accent. And He is addressing *her:* an enemy, a woman, a sinner. She swings around to see who is asking her for a drink of water.

He looks like a Jewish rabbi. Her mind reels, trying to process the irony. Then He offers her a mysterious source of water that will never dry up. She doesn't completely understand, but she knows she wants some of *that* water. Then comes the downer: when she asks for the water, He tells her to go get her husband. She has to confess that she doesn't have one. Technically, that is true; she's had five and is now living with a man who isn't her husband. Somehow, the rabbi knows all about it. This blows her mind.

Trying to change the subject, she asks Him a question she has heard debated for years—a theological question about how people should worship God. The rabbi tells her that worship doesn't focus on a place, but on God himself. Her mind starts swimming again. Then she expresses her hope that some day the promised Messiah will come and make sense of it all. Jesus responds, "I am He."

She can't take the excitement. She drops her jug and runs full tilt toward town to tell everyone that the Messiah, the Savior of the world, is there at the well, outside their little town. Even today, her exuberant message resounds.

The Word Speaks

Have one person from the group read aloud **John 4:4-15**.

The Samaritan people were a racial mixture produced through the intermarrying of Israelites with their Assyrian captors during one of the darkest times of Jewish history. Purebred Jews shunned the Samaritans, even rejecting their help to rebuild the temple in Nehemiah's day. So the Samaritans built a rival temple on Mount Gerizim. Pious Jews painstakingly avoided contact with Samaritans, to the point of detouring several miles around Samaritan territory when traveling from Judea to Galilee. What light does this background information shed on the context of Jesus' conversation with this woman at the well?

Did You Know?

There was another well (the *'Ain 'Askar*), on the east side of the little town, and much nearer to Sychar than "Jacob's Well"; and to it probably the women of Sychar generally resorted . . . This Samaritaness may have chosen "Jacob's Well," perhaps . . . because, if her character was what seems implied in John 4:18, the concourse of the more common women at the village-well of an evening might scarcely be a pleasant place of resort.

—Alfred Edersheim

Read the note about Jacob's Well. Then comment on why this woman might have gone to the farther-away well, at an unusual hour of the day. Why would this multiply her surprise that a Jewish *man* would deign to speak to her?

How does this help you understand her intense desire for the water Jesus offered—the kind that would make it unnecessary for her to come to the well every day? How is His water infinitely more valuable?

Now, read **John 4:16-26**, and **28-30**.

Why do you suppose the woman deflected the conversation away from her marital status and toward a theological issue?

Read the quote from *Nelson's New Illustrated Bible Commentary*. Then scan Jesus' clandestine conversation with Nicodemus in John 3:1–21. Why do you suppose this woman was so quick to accept Jesus as the long-awaited deliverer? Contrast her immediate response with Nicodemus' hesitancy and the secrecy of his discipleship (John 7:50–53; 19:39–42) until after Jesus' crucifixion.

Read the note from the *Believer's Bible Commentary*. In light of the woman's response, why do you suppose Jesus was able to use this opportunity to directly and clearly state His true identity? How does this differ from the cryptic way He usually identified himself as the Son of Man?

Why was it natural for the woman to drop her water jar and race to the city to tell the men and women there the best news she'd ever heard?

What Others Say

The Judeans rejected the testimony of their own Scriptures, John the Baptist, and Christ's miracles and teachings. The Samaritans accepted the testimony of an outcast woman. Sometimes God uses the most unlikely source to accomplish His work, while those who should have been at the forefront of the work of God fail to follow Him.

—*Nelson's New Illustrated Bible Commentary*

Bible Background

What Jesus said to her was literally, "I who speak to you am." The word *He* is not a part of the original text . . . In using the words "I am" He used one of the names which God applied to Himself in the Old Testament . . . He was announcing to her the startling truth that the One who was speaking to her was the Messiah for whom she had been looking and that He was also God Himself.

—Believer's Bible Commentary

Finally, have someone read **John 4:39-42**. After meditating on these verses silently, recall the name of the person who introduced you to Jesus and the circumstances of your conversion. At what point did you make your belief your own, rather than simply trusting someone else's testimony?

Where We Come In

If Jesus were to visibly step into your room, what questions would you ask Him? What hidden sins might He identify, and how might you be tempted to deflect His attention away from them? If He recognized your sin and offered you true forgiveness and strength to conquer your sin, what would you do?

How It Works Today

This is the testimony of Christian writer Beth Abeyta:

"Although I had been raised Catholic, I didn't know I needed a personal relationship with Jesus to be cleansed of my sins. During my teenage years, I read books that lead me to the occult, New Age, and witchcraft. I followed these leads, which did nothing to satisfy the desire I had for deep, abiding love. My feeling of loss was amplified when, after a two-year marriage, I found myself divorced at age twenty-two. I was looking to my husband to fulfill me in ways only God could.

At this point I was taking classes at a community college and was befriended by one of my teachers, who turned out to be a pastor. He seemed 'too cool' to be a preacher, but his intelligence, charisma, and genuine caring drew me. By the time he shared the gospel with me, it seemed so right and clear that I couldn't believe it took me so long to realize its truth."

What does it mean to you that Jesus said His Father is seeking true worshippers—those who worship Him in spirit and in truth? How does this shake up your previous notions of worship?

Read Revelation 4:8–11, which describes worship in heaven. Listen as the creatures and the elders express their worship. How does this help you focus your attempts to worship God? How does your worship experience align with this heavenly model?

In what ways does your chosen place of worship help you focus your attention on Him? How can a place of worship become a hindrance to true worship?

Read the story about Beth Abeyta. How did Beth's professor testify to the life-changing power of Jesus? How did he draw her attention to Christ?

Whom do you need to run to and tell about your personal encounter with Jesus? What are the water jugs in your life that keep you from running freely with the amazing message that God has visited this planet and made a way for mere mortals to have eternal companionship with Him? How can you get rid of them?

What Others Say

I suspect some of us would rather die before we missed our lunch in order to do something for God! Jesus . . . was on earth to talk to men and women about himself. That was why he took time out—even when he was tired and hungry—to explain the things of God to a rather disreputable lady.

—Jill Briscoe

Read the quote by Jill Briscoe. How do you respond to her indictment of our unwillingness to be inconvenienced by serving God? What opportunities have you missed because your fatigue or everyday demands took priority? What do you wish you would have done instead? What will you do next time?

Responding through Prayer

As you pray today, invite God to reveal himself so clearly to you that you will worship Him wholeheartedly, not only in formal, corporate worship, but by doing His will with every breath of life.

My Next Step

This week I will:

- Be on the lookout for God's prompting to tell others about Him—even when it doesn't feel convenient or comfortable for me to do so.

-

-

Keep It in Mind

Each day this week, read the proclamation of the Samaritans: "We have heard for ourselves, and we know that this man really is the Savior of the world" (John 4:42). Remind yourself that this Savior of the world is your personal Lord and Savior and determine to worship Him in spirit and in truth.

7

Caught and Released

John 7:53–8:12

"Teacher, this woman was caught in the act of adultery. In the Law Moses commanded us to stone such women. Now what do you say?" When they kept on questioning him, he straightened up and said to them, "If any one of you is without sin, let him be the first to throw a stone at her."

—John 8:5, 7

Discovery

A true glimpse of Jesus transforms our own self-image.

For Openers

We've all fallen into sin's trap. There isn't one of us who hasn't succumbed at one time or another to the sin of shading the truth to make ourselves look better, of embellishing stories about someone else to tear them down, of taking what isn't ours to use for our own benefit, or of covering up our faults so others will think we are without sin.

Like a persistent telephone, ringing and ringing, sin calls. And we answer. We almost can't help ourselves. It is in our nature to do wrong—to fall short of the perfect goal God sets before us. One mistake and we've missed the mark entirely. We are utterly and unabashedly guilty. But through Christ we are declared innocent and given the ability to live in victory over sin.

We will confront many sins in today's story. Overt sins like that of the woman we'll meet (and the man we won't); and covert sins such as the underlying arrogance, power-mongering, and self-righteousness that motivates the religious rulers.

We also will confront the One who has the right to stone every last sinner to death. But instead of using His hands to bruise sinners, we'll watch as He uses them to write mysterious messages in a patch of desert sand, and listen as He speaks a message of holiness that challenges us today in our own sinful lives.

Getting to Know Her

Interruptions. Entrapment. Misquoting and manipulating the Scriptures they claim to scrupulously uphold. Taunting and over-ruling voices among their own ranks that call for a reasoned response to the Teacher. The downward sin-spiral of the Jewish leaders is blatant and manipulative.

They devise ways to disgrace Jesus publicly because He is supplanting their authority with the "ignorant" crowds. This time they set a trap with a woman who has succumbed to the sin of adultery. Can you sense her flailing in the trap?

They yank this woman down to the temple courts, blustering their way into the middle of Jesus' teaching, and present her with an accusation: "We caught her in the act of adultery. Moses tells us to stone her. What do you say?" *Get yourself out of this one, Teacher.*

Jesus infuriates them by bending down and writing in the sand, not saying a word. When they continue to yell despite His controlled silence, He stands to His full height and looks them in the eye. "Go ahead; stone her," He tells them. You can hear the boulders emerging from within the folds of their robes as they prepare to hurl. "But the first stone must be cast by the one among you who has never sinned," He continues before stooping to write more in the sand.

One by one the religious leaders slowly walk away as the stones they have been holding tightly, softly thud against the ground.

The Word Speaks
Silently read **John 7:53-8:12**.

As you reach verse 6, pause for at least one minute before moving on to the remainder of the passage. Listen in the silence for God's word to you.

Share with the group (or write in your journal) the impressions you had as you waited between verses 6 and 7 to hear God speak to you.

Read the "Bible Background" note about the Scriptural basis for the religious leaders' claim. Why do you suppose they manipulated the Scriptures for their own purposes? What does the part they conveniently excluded (that the man is equally responsible and equally to be punished) tell you about God's justice?

Bible Background

The law the Pharisees were quoting in part would have come from Leviticus 20:10, which reads, "If a man commits adultery with another man's wife—with the wife of his neighbor—both the adulterer and the adulteress must be put to death." It isn't just the woman who must be put to death (and stoning isn't even mentioned here), but the man, too, is under the same punishment.

Read the quote from S. P. and L. Richards. How does this succinct explanation add to your understanding of the woman's plight and the motives of the religious leaders?

Turn your attention to the woman. Experience her range of emotions: panic, fear, pain, shame, and relief. Imagine how she felt as she heard Jesus tell them to stone her. Imagine her confusion when He added the qualification about who could toss the first stone. Why do you suppose she didn't run away when the

What Others Say

Guilty men had dragged a guilty woman before the One Person who knew the hearts of all: the One Person who had entered the world not to condemn sinners, but to save them.

—S. P. and L. Richards

accusers departed? What does it say about her heart that she stayed to await Jesus' words—and her penalty?

Read the quote by songwriter and author Michael Card. What divine revelation might have come from those "scratches and scribbles in the sand"? Comment on the notion that the same finger that "traced the galaxies" busied itself on this day scribbling in the sand.

What Others Say

The One who had traced the galaxies with that same finger, hunched over like a schoolboy, his tongue perhaps protruding from the corner of his mouth, writing once more those words we would give a treasure to know but never will . . . From the flat, gray point of view of the fallen world they are only scratches and scribbles in the sand, but in the light of eternity they become the occasion for divine revelation.

—Michael Card

Did You Know?

[The passage] 7:53 through 8:11 does not appear in the most ancient [manuscripts] of John, but is found in over 900 Greek [manuscripts] (the vast majority) . . . We believe that it is proper to accept them as part of the inspired text. All that they teach is in perfect agreement with the rest of the Bible.

—Believer's Bible Commentary

Where We Come In

Read the note from the *Believer's Bible Commentary*. Why do you think this passage is included in Scripture? How do you respond to Augustine's explanation for its temporary exclusion in the early years? Is Jesus' forgiveness cheap for the woman? Do His words promote "loose views on morality," or do they offer motivation and ability to turn from sin? How so?

Of all those gathered there, only Jesus had the right to throw that first stone. He was the only one without sin. Why does this make a difference in the story? What does it say about God's right to punish you? What does it say about His inclination to do so?

What alternative does God offer for the deserved punishment of the guilty? What are the requirements for those who seek forgiveness? How would you explain to another sinner the way to receive forgiveness, as well as the reason to ask for it?

What sin in your life would you be ashamed for Jesus to confront? Imagine Him standing face to face with you, watching your face as your enemies proclaim that sin to a watching world. Hear His words

How It Works Today

Daniele lived in the slums of Brazil. She was eleven years old when her stepfather raped her, injuring her so badly that she was hospitalized. When she left the hospital, Daniele was no longer welcome in her mother's home, so she took to the streets, delivering for a drug dealer. When she told her dealer about the rape, the dealer became so enraged that he kidnapped the man, gave Daniele a gun, and instructed her to shoot her stepfather. She obeyed.

The authorities placed Daniele in a correction home. At age twelve she escaped to live on the streets again. At fourteen she was placed in a Christ-centered transition home known as Reencontro outside Rio de Janeiro. Believers there reunited Daniele with her mother and introduced them to Christ. Mother and daughter believed and were discipled; both chose to make the most of this second chance to rebuild their lives.

to you, "Neither do I condemn you. Go and stop sinning." What sins might He be identifying in your life? How do you intend to respond?

Because the Law of Moses did give the religious leaders the right to kill the woman as punishment for the sin she was caught committing, she was as good as dead. She had no recourse. Yet Jesus offered her a clean slate so she could start over. When has He done that for you? Share with the group a time when He forgave you and offered you the opportunity to start fresh. Explain what you did with that opportunity.

Read the story about Daniele. How can Christian believers offer a second chance to those who are hurting, lost, alone, or ready to give in? Who in your world needs a second chance? How will you approach that person? What do you have to offer that can help her turn from sin?

Why do you suppose this passage closes with Jesus' words about being the light of the world? How does darkness confront light in this woman's life? How does it confront light in your life? Ultimately, which will win?

Responding through Prayer

As you pray, begin by confessing your sins to Christ and accepting the forgiveness He offers through His shed blood. Hear Him challenge you to go and stop sinning. Decide to obey. Finally, ask Him to bring to mind someone who needs this same forgiveness from Him.

My Next Step

This week I will initiate contact with the following people, who need God's grace, and show them (gently) what a difference Jesus has made in my life:

-
-

Keep It in Mind

As a reminder to look for ways Jesus is revealing himself to you, keep this Scripture passage close at hand this week: "I am the light of the world. Whoever follows me will never walk in darkness, but will have the light of life" (John 8:12).

8

The Miracle of Christ's Compassion

Luke 13:10–17

A woman was there who . . . was bent over and could not straighten up at all. When Jesus saw her, he called her forward and said to her, "Woman, you are set free from your infirmity." Then he put his hands on her, and immediately she straightened up and praised God.

—Luke 13:11–13

Discovery

Worshipping God brings unexpected transformation.

For Openers

Good news! We can now buy a carbonated soft drink enhanced and enriched with, among other tasty treats, calcium. Yum. I don't know about you, but I drink carbonated beverages to get a daily fix of empty calories and a jolt of caffeine. Make it good for me, give it a redeeming value, and it loses its charm.

So, you agree that enriched cola isn't your thing? You can also get calcium from enriched orange juice, oatmeal bars, cereal, cookies, even chocolates. Why this mega-effort to up our calcium intakes? Osteoporosis. We've all seen loved ones "lose an inch" as they age because of this disease. And we have seen others deformed by a curvature of the spine known as kyphosis, a result of osteoporosis-fractured vertebrae. Medical professionals recommend we up our intake of calcium to limit the likelihood of the disease—and we listen because it's a disease we'd like to avoid.

The woman we'll meet today suffered from kyphosis. Jesus' prescription for her, however, was different than what today's medical establishment would call for. It isn't that Jesus didn't know about calcium's benefits; He had a more complete healing in mind, and an important purpose to accomplish through this woman's need. Through her, He demonstrated His awareness of the pain in each of our lives, and His willingness to offer us the freedom we crave.

Getting to Know Her

Jesus is heading to Jerusalem to die. But the disciples and the religious leaders have lessons yet to learn. And Jesus has lives yet to transform. As He travels, He regularly infuriates the leaders by exposing their motivations as empty, vain, and downright evil.

At one moment Jesus looks across the synagogue where He is teaching on the Sabbath and sees a woman who has been in agony for more than eighteen years. Her back is crumpled with osteoporosis, and she can't straighten up at all.

Imagine the pain and the humiliation the woman has endured. Yet, she is in the synagogue on the Sabbath, preparing to worship. She doesn't approach Jesus; she doesn't ask for anything. She is there, as she has been all of her life, to give homage to God.

But Jesus calls to her, giving her value. He touches her with the very hands of God. Imagine the electricity that traverses her spine the instant the Creator's hands touch her—the unbridled excitement as she feels vertebrae realign and strength return to the surrounding muscles.

No longer the object of physical torture, spiritual mocking, or man's scorn, she can hold her head high. She can stand tall. She can look into Jesus' eyes. And her first response? Gratitude, worship, and awe—all directed toward the God who had mercy on her.

Immediately, the synagogue leader harangues Jesus for healing her on *that* day. "Aren't there six other days to heal?" he yells at the people. "Why does this man flout the rules and work on the Sabbath?"

Then Jesus, the Word who spoke the Sabbath into existence, responds that doing good on the Sabbath is not only allowed but encouraged. This elicits raucous laughter from the crowd, and more infuriation from the religious leaders.

The Word Speaks

Listen as a volunteer reads **Luke 13:10-17** aloud. Picture the scene in your mind's eye, as if you were watching it transpire on a movie screen.

Put yourself in the shoes of one of the people in the crowd that day. Go through the emotions you would have experienced as an observer. Pay special attention to the statement in verse 17.

After rereading Luke's description of the scene, put yourself in the place of the woman who was healed. What would you have experienced from the moment you stepped into the synagogue until the moment you strode home, straight and tall?

Reread verse 14. Why do you suppose the synagogue ruler yelled his accusation to the crowd rather than directing his question toward Jesus? What response do you suppose he was hoping to warrant?

How does it encourage you to know that the woman didn't have to justify Jesus' actions on her behalf and the disciples didn't have to answer for Him—rather, Jesus answered the ruler head on?

How is this man's attitude toward Jesus different than that of another synagogue ruler, Jairus (Mark 5)? What might be some reasons for the differences?

Bible Background

When God gave the commandment to dedicate the seventh day as holy, He appears to have intended it as a time for refreshing rest from the labor of the week, and as sweet hours of communion with Him.

Read the "Bible Background" note. Then read Exodus 20:8–11 and note the reasons God lists for this special day. Compare Exodus 20:8–11 with Jesus' words in Luke 13:15–16. Does the ruler have a valid point about keeping the Sabbath?

Read the quote by S. P. Richards, and consider the perspective of the religious leaders. What can this part of the story help you infer about the ruler's character and his reason for raising the question? Do you suppose he really was concerned about the purity of the Sabbath?

What Others Say

The bent woman's frailty revealed the hard-heartedness of the religious leaders.

—S. P. Richards

Read the quote by Archibald Thomas Robertson. What does this suggest about how Christ would have us treat those among us who are dealing with chronic pain?

Did You Know?

His words have a ludicrous sound as if all the people had to do to get their crooked backs straightened out was to come round to his synagogue during the week. He forgot that this poor old woman had been coming for eighteen years with no result.

—Archibald Thomas Robertson

Read 1 Corinthians 1:27–29. Note the contrasts Paul sets up in this passage, and consider why God often works in unexpected ways. How does understanding this passage help you put this woman's story into context?

Where We Come In

Glance back through the text. The woman did not approach Jesus. He saw her, called her, had mercy on her, and acted swiftly to identify her need and heal her completely—and publicly. When you think of the value Jesus places on this daughter of Abraham, what can you conclude about the value He also places on you as an individual? How does this make you feel? He knows about your challenges and difficult circumstances, and He cares. How might He be seeking you out to meet your needs?

Consider the words of Jesus in Luke 19:10. In what ways did He seek and save this unnamed woman? In what ways has He sought and saved you? How does His pursuit of you give you value?

How It Works Today

Mrs. Volpi was a good friend's grandmother. As we shared holiday meals, I studied her attentive eyes, shrinking posture, arthritic hands, and slightly faltering voice. She was a living history, a link back to a time when her family and mine had come to Christ.

Mrs. Volpi's father pastored a church early in the twentieth century. Like her parents, she became a faithful Christ-follower. As an adolescent, she began her role as church pianist. Every service, for many decades, she took her seat at the keyboard and helped lead worship. When osteoporosis robbed her of height and bone strength, and arthritis robbed her of dexterity, even then she continued to serve Christ through music and through her regular presence in worship services.

When finally she needed more medical care than her family could offer, they moved her to a lovely hotel-like residential care facility. There Mrs. Volpi found a piano and began to play old hymns for her fellow residents. And so she continued expressing worship to God through piano keys until her final days.

Read the story about Mrs. Volpi. What does the lifelong faithfulness to God of a woman like Mrs. Volpi challenge you to do for God with your talents—despite your limitations?

Consider the Sabbath command again. Why is it significant that Jesus' concern for an individual woman superseded a legalistic interpretation of the commandment? Name a time when legalism got in the way of your relationship with Him. How did you get past it?

How does the spirit of the Sabbath-command apply to the way we spend our week? What does the idea of a true Sabbath say about how God values you as an individual and how He values your relationship with Him? What does it say about the balance between a relationship *with* Him and what you do *for* Him?

Consider that God knows about your pain and is ready to meet your deepest need. If Jesus were to walk into your room today, what need would He recognize in you? Share that need with someone you trust, and agree to make it a matter of prayer this week. When He comes to you and meets that need—whether today or tomorrow or farther in the future, don't forget to do as the woman did—give glory and praise to God.

Responding through Prayer

Individually, silently say this prayer: *God, it encourages my heart to know how gently You came to the hurting woman in this story and how You met her need. Like this woman, I have a need only You can meet. I need Your touch in the area of . . .*

Would You come to me, even as I am here worshipping You and learning from Your Word? Thank You for showing me how much you value me.

My Next Step

I will remind myself each day this week that my pain touches Jesus and that He cares. Therefore, I will have the confidence to:

Keep It in Mind

Keep this Scripture passage close at hand in the coming week, as both a reminder and a challenge: "And my God will meet all your needs according to his glorious riches in Christ Jesus" (Phil. 4:19).